SandCastle 2

Baby Animals

Kittens

Kelly Doudna

ABDO
Publishing Company

Z0062017

Published by SandCastle™, an imprint of ABDO Publishing Company, 4940 Viking Drive, Edina, Minnesota 55435.

Printed in the United States.

Photo credits: Walter Rohdich; Frank Lane Picture Agency/Corbis, James Marshall/Corbis, Michael Boys/©Corbis, Paul A. Souders/©Corbis, Digital Stock, Kelly Doudna, John Foxx Images

Library of Congress Cataloging-in-Publication Data

Doudna, Kelly, 1963-
    Kittens / Kelly Doudna.
       p. cm. -- (Baby animals)
    Summary: Simple text and photographs present the physical characteristics and behavior of kittens.
    ISBN 1-57765-182-0
    1. Kittens--Juvenile literature. [1. Cats: 2. Animals--Infancy.] I. Title. II. Series: Doudna, Kelly, 1963- Baby animals.
SF445.7.D68 1999
636.8'07--DC21
                                       98-21703
                                          CIP
                                          AC

The SandCastle concept, content, and reading method have been reviewed and approved by a national advisory board including literacy specialists, librarians, elementary school teachers, early childhood education professionals, and parents.

Let Us Know

After reading the book, SandCastle would like you to tell us your stories about reading. What is your favorite page? Was there something hard that you needed help with? Share the ups and downs of learning to read. We want to hear from you! To get posted on the Abdo Publishing Company Web site, send us email at:

sandcastle@abdopub.com

About SandCastle™
Nonfiction books for the beginning reader

- Basic concepts of phonics are incorporated with integrated language methods of reading instruction. Most words are short, and phrases, letter sounds, and word sounds are repeated.

- Readability is determined by the number of words in each sentence, the number of characters in each word, and word lists based on curriculum frameworks.

- Full-color photography reinforces word meanings and concepts.

- "Words I Can Read" list at the end of each book teaches basic elements of grammar, helps the reader recognize the words in the text, and builds vocabulary.

- Reading levels are indicated by the number of flags on the castle.

Look for more SandCastle books in these three reading levels:

Level 1 (one flag)	Level 2 (two flags)	Level 3 (three flags)
Grades Pre-K to K	**Grades K to 1**	**Grades 1 to 2**
5 or fewer words per page	5 to 10 words per page	10 to 15 words per page

A young cat is
a kitten.

Kittens are small.

These kittens are
brothers and sisters.

This kitten lives on
a farm.

This kitten rests in
the woods.

This kitten plays
with a green ball.

This kitten is scared.

It tries to look big.

This kitten had
a bath.

It is wet.

This kitten looks
at a big dog.

This kitten plays outside.

Do you?

Words I Can Read

Nouns

A noun is a person, place, or thing

ball (BAWL) p. 13
bath (BATH) p. 17
cat (KAT) p. 5
dog (DAWG) p. 19
farm (FARM) p. 9
kitten (KIT-uhn)
pp. 5, 9, 11, 13, 15, 17, 19, 21

Plural Nouns

A plural noun is more than one
person, place, or thing

brothers (BRUHTH-urz) p. 7
kittens (KIT-uhnz) pp. 5, 7
sisters (SISS-turz) p. 7
woods (WUDZ) p. 11

Verbs

A verb is an action or being word

are (AR) pp. 5, 7
do (DOO) p. 21
had (HAD) p. 17
is (IZ) pp. 5, 15, 17
lives (LIVZ) p. 9
look (LUK) p. 15
looks (LUKSS) p. 19
plays (PLAYZ) pp. 13, 21
rests (RESTSS) p. 11
tries (TRYZ) p. 15

Adjectives

An adjective describes something

big (BIG) p. 19
green (GREEN) p. 13
scared (SKAIRD) p. 15
small (SMAWL) p. 5
wet (WET) p. 17
young (YUHNG) p. 5

Sight Words

barn

farm

dog

woods